IDEAL PROPERTIES OF A FINANCIAL CRYPTOGRAPHIC SYSTEM

COMPUTATIONAL AND LEGAL ASPECTS

ERIC ENGLE

Copyright © 2018

http://www.amazon.com/author/quizmaster

http://mindworks.altervista.org

Introduction

I wrote this book to explain optimal cryptographic protocols for digital currency and the laws which underpin digital finance. Knowing cryptography and law enables digital startups and investors to understand the limits and possibilities of crypto-currency. This knowledge also enables creation of legal semi-anonymous crypto-currency to enable micro-credit for legitimate purposes in cash-poor under-developed economies.

Failed states, for example Zimbabwe, often are governed by kleptocratic elites. Ruinous inflationary financial policies, selective taxation, fines, rampant bribery, and outright expropriation explain why under-developed countries are so poor. Private digital currency can enable poor rural farmers to escape from barter increasing economic efficiency. Private digital currency will also enable micro-credit to the impoverished.

Digital currency also presents obvious opportunities for investors. This book presents cryptographically secure protocols for legally provable digital financial instruments: claims which can be proven before courts of law and equity.

A Fulbright law specialist, I have taught law in a half dozen countries and published dozens of articles and books about business law and computer science. I hope you will enjoy this book and find it useful.

Table of Contents

Introduction 2

1. Introduction 7

    1.1 Cryptographic Conventions 7

    1.2 Illegal Uses of Digital Currency 8

    1.3 Legitimate Uses for Crypto-Currency 9

2. Code and Cipher Systems 10

    2.1 Codes 10

    2.2 Steganography - Visual, Audio 11

    2.3 Ciphers 12

        2.3.1 Substitution Ciphers ("Caesar Cipher"): Monoalphabetic 12

        2.3.2 Polyalphabetic Substitution Ciphers (Usually, "Vigenere") 13

        2.3.3 Asymmetric Cryptography (Usually, "Public Key") 15

        2.3.4 One Way Functions 16

        2.3.5 Transposition Ciphers 18

        2.3.6 One Time Pads 19

    2.4 Cryptographic Vulnerabilities 22

3. Elements of Rebus Ciphers ... 23

   3.1 Pictorial Elements of Rebus ... 24

   3.2 Semantic Elements of Rebus ... 26

   3.3 Phonetic Elements of Rebus ... 27

   3.4 Rebus Characters' Structure ... 29

   3.5 Transliteration using Romanization ... 30

4. Ideal Properties of a Digital Payment System ... 31

5. Legal Aspects of Crypto Currency: Problems and Possibilities ... 37

   5.1 Problems Facing Legal Enforcement of crypto-currency Transactions ... 38

      5.1.1 Equity Unavailable for Crypto-Currency Claims ... 39

      5.1.2 In Pari Delicto ... 40

      5.1.3 Statute of Frauds ... 40

      5.1.4 Courts Refuse to Enforce or Remedy Illegal Contracts ... 41

   5.2 Possibilities of Lawful Enforceable Digital Financial Instruments ... 42

      5.2.1 Commercial Paper (Negotiable Instruments) ... 42

      5.2.2 Intellectual Property ... 44

5.2.2.1 Patent	44
5.2.2.2 Trade Secret	45
5.2.2.3 Trademark	45
5.2.2.4 Recordation	46
5.2.2.5 Choice of Law Clauses	46
Conclusion	48
About The Author	49
Other Books By Eric Engle	50
References	52

1. Introduction

Current financial cryptographic systems rely on asymmetric public key encryption. These cryptographic systems may not be as secure as is believed and suffer from certain weaknesses, some but not all of which are inevitable to any cryptographic system. Meanwhile, several legal concerns undermine the viability of crypto-currency as a financial instrument Herein I propose an alternative cryptographic protocol for digital payments to enable legitimate economic functions of digital currency while evading risks of illegality to digital currency. I also discuss some of the legal problems facing crypto-currencies like bitcoin.

1.1 Cryptographic Conventions

Financial cryptology is a subset of cryptology. Much of the same nomenclature and methods can be applied to financial cryptology as are used in other branches of cryptology. For example, in cryptology we generally speak of two parties to a conversation, "Alice" and "Bob", who are being listened to by third parties conventionally called "Charlie" and or "Eve" (the eavesdropper). In financial cryptography instead of speaking of "Alice", "Bob", "Charlie" and "Eve" we can refer to these roles more specifically as "Drawer", "Payee", "Emitter", and "thiEVEs".

1.2 Illegal Uses of Digital Currency

It is fairly obvious that there are numerous illicit uses of digital currency: money laundering, tax evasion, but also drug dealing and human trafficking. I have extensively examined the problems of illegality in crypto-currency in an earlier book, including counterfeit and stock fraud aspects.[1] In this book I instead consider legal aspects of crypto-currency with a view to developing lawful digital financial instruments which may be plead, proven, and enforced before courts of law and equity. Rather than look at securities regulations and counterfeiting as my earlier book did here I consider rules of private contract law rather than public criminal law to enable lawful digital financial instruments. Crypto-currency as currently conceived is regularly used for illegal transactions and therefore is in the long run unsustainable. New better ideas are needed.

1.3 Legitimate Uses for Crypto-Currency

Although bitcoin is associated rightly with drug dealing, human trafficking, and tax evasion, there are also legitimate reasons and lawful uses for digital currency. Digital currency may enable micro-credit loans and trade between the very poorest people on earth who have access neither to cash or credit and thus must inefficiently barter the few goods they have. These people moreover are often the victims of human trafficking or debt slavery (indenture). Meanwhile, kleptocracies often face underdevelopment because kleptocratic inflation, kleptocratic asset seizure, and selective taxation all stunt economic growth. Digital currency can enable capital expatriation from kleptocratic regimes or enable the creation of an alternative domestic economy to avoid the worst features of kleptocracy in failed states like Zimbabwe. Finally, the suppression of political dissidents explains why digital crypto-currency can be a useful tool against tyranny, whether to fund, reward, or extract political dissidents from failed states. Micro-credit, kleptocracy, hyperinflation, and political dissidence all explain why digital crypto-currency can, under certain exceptional circumstances, be desirable.

I explicit certain cryptographic methods and laws here to enable creation of a semi-anonymous crypto-currency for these legitimate purposes.

2. CODE AND CIPHER SYSTEMS

The various encoding and enciphering systems used in military cryptography can be applied to the field of financial cryptography. This section provides a brief explanation of cryptographic methods for digital finance. It is intended as a primer for those relatively unaware of cryptography.

2.1 CODES

A code book, properly speaking, is a dictionary of terms with their corresponding plain text definitions. A brief example illustrates:

```
Big bird = President
Midsky   = 12 Noon
Chirps   = Talks, Speaks
D.C.     = Aviary
```

So the coded text "Big bird chirps at midsky in the aviary on 4 April" would decode as "The President speaks at noon on April 4th in Washington D.C."

This code is obviously not too strong. Intuitively we might understand "chirping" as speaking, an "aviary" is a place where "birds" "nest" and that a "big bird" is an important "bird". Recall that "bird" is a slang term for colonel. However, a well drafted code might look like "Tomato is three" or "Purple jeans table bread" or any other nonsense (including alphanumeric strings).

Well-drafted code-books are on their own terms unbreakable. They resulting encoded texts are however vulnerable to stylometry and physical attacks. If the code-book falls into enemy hands then the code is compromised. The solution to these problems is very large code books (many terms, i.e. dictionary length) used to transmit only short messages and frequent changing of the code book. A code is, in principle, computationally secure.

2.2 Steganography - visual, audio

Steganography is the use of one medium to mask another message. The mask is usually a picture or image. The message is somehow hidden within the image or sound. The actual message can be extracted from the steganograph.

2.3 Ciphers

Ciphers are the most widely known form of encryption. I discuss symmetric ciphers first. In a symmetric cipher the same key is used to encipher and decipher the information. We proceed from simplest ciphers to most complex with the understanding that the more complex systems tended to develop out of the simpler systems and thus this primer presents the various ciphers in roughly historical progression.

2.3.1 Substitution Ciphers ("Caesar Cipher"): Monoalphabetic

The simplest cipher is a substitution cipher where e.g. A=1 B=2 C=3 etc. Thus, "Eric" enciphers as
5 18 13 9 3.
These types of ciphers are known as monoalphabetic substitution ciphers. The next step in complexity is to use a key number to shift the initial key: The substitution may be assigned a "shift" value (decalage). For example, if we have a monoalphabetic substitution cipher with a shift of one, then the encrypted values become
6 19 14 10 4.
This is called a monoalphabetic cipher because each letter in the cipher text corresponds to one, and only one, plain

text letter. Of course we can and often do use letters instead of numbers. Greater complexity can be achieved in a monoalphabetic cipher by using a key which is not in alphabetic order. For example,

ABCDEFGHIJKLMNOPQRSTUVWXYZ - Plain text
FEDCONUSAGMTHBKILJPNWOZYVX - Key

In this example
ERIC enciphers to
OJAD. This is however still a monoalphabetic cipher: E in this example always enciphers to O and O always deciphers to E, for example.

2.3.2 POLYALPHABETIC SUBSTITUTION CIPHERS (USUALLY, "VIGENERE")

In a polyalphabetic cipher different letters of the plain-text may encipher to more than one letter in the cipher key. Keyed Vigenere is the most famous polyalphabetic substitution cipher and probably also the most secure cipher capable of being hand enciphered (which isn't saying much). So for example with the alphabet key:

ANNUITCOEPTIS

we obtain this tableau of substitutions:

	ANUI	TCOE	PSBD	FGHJ	KLMQ	RVWX	YZ
A	ANUI	TCOE	PSBD	FGHJ	KLMQ	RVWX	YZ
N	NUIT	COEP	SBDF	GHJK	LMQR	VWXY	ZA
U	UITC	OEPS	BDFG	HJKL	MQRV	WXYZ	AN
I	ITCO	EPSB	DFGH	JKLM	QRVW	XYZA	NU
T	TCOE	PSBD	FGHJ	KLMQ	RVWX	YZAN	UI
C	COEP	SBDF	GHJK	LMQR	VWXY	ZANU	IT
O	OEPS	BDFG	HJKL	MQRV	WXYZ	ANUI	TC
E	EPSB	DFGH	JKLM	QRVW	XYZA	NUIT	CO
P	PSBD	FGHJ	KLMQ	RVWX	YZAN	UITC	OE
S	SBDF	GHJK	LMQR	VWXY	ZANU	ITCO	EP
B	BDFG	HJKL	MQRV	WXYZ	ANUI	TCOE	PS
D	DFGH	JKLM	QRVW	XYZA	NUIT	COEP	SB
F	FGHJ	KLMQ	RVWX	YZAN	UITC	OEPS	BD
G	GHJK	LMQR	VWXY	ZANU	ITCO	EPSB	DF
H	HJKL	MQRV	WXYZ	ANUI	TCOE	PSBD	FG
J	JKLM	QRVW	XYZA	NUIT	COEP	SBDF	GH
K	KLMQ	RVWX	YZAN	UITC	OEPS	BDFG	HJ
L	LMQR	VWXY	ZANU	ITCO	EPSB	DFGH	JK
M	MQRV	WXYZ	ANUI	TCOE	PSBD	FGHJ	KL
Q	QRVW	XYZA	NUIT	COEP	SBDF	GHJK	LM
R	RVWX	YZAN	UITC	OEPS	BDFG	HJKL	MQ
V	VWXY	ZANU	ITCO	EPSB	DFGH	JKLM	QR
W	WXYZ	ANUI	TCOE	PSBD	FGHJ	KLMQ	RV
X	XYZA	NUIT	COEP	SBDF	GHJK	LMQR	VW
Y	YZAN	UITC	OEPS	BDFG	HJKL	MQRV	WX
Z	ZANU	ITCO	EPSB	DFGH	JKLM	QRVW	XY

which are then further indexed using the passphrase

NOVUSORDOSAECLORUM

To encipher the plain-text message:
GIVE ME YOUR TIRED YOUR POOR YOUR HUDDLED MASSES

yielding:
HSKS NG MLPI TBZYL MPRV HNPI TAGA XUMKPGC RMBJUD
as the cipher-text.

Note that YOUR here enciphers first as MLPI and then as MPRV. This is the feature which makes a polyalphabetic cipher stronger than a monoalphabetic substitution: one letter may encipher into two different letters.

2.3.3 ASYMMETRIC CRYPTOGRAPHY (USUALLY, "PUBLIC KEY")

So far we have only discussed symmetric key cryptography. In a symmetric key system the same key is used to both encipher and decipher the text. Symmetric systems necessarily require private keys.

Symmetric key cryptography must be distinguished from asymmetric cryptography. In asymmetric cryptography two different keys are used. One key is to encipher the text, and another key is used to decipher the text. This permits a wide or even public dissemination of the key used to encipher. Provided the private key is kept truly private, asymmetric cryptography is generally regarded as computationally secure. Public key cryptography is a form of asymmetric cryptography wherein a party holds a private key which may easily decipher messages and issues a public key which can readily encipher messages but cannot directly decipher messages. To form a secure public key requires a one way function so that the private key cannot readily be derived from the public key.

2.3.4 ONE WAY FUNCTIONS

The principle behind public key cryptography is that some mathematical functions are easy to compute one way but are difficult to reverse. The usual function used to generate key pairs in public key cryptography is factorization of primes. It is easy to multiply two very large primes. Yet it is difficult to determine the prime factors of the resulting composite number. This is because the number of digits in the primes used are known and smaller than the number of digits in the resulting composite number. Supposedly, one way functions have not been proven to exist. In fact however, since the factorization of a very large prime requires testing each number smaller than the composite to determine if it is one of the factors it is evident that indeed factorization of primes is a one way function. If we take two small primes as an example 3 and 13 we can in one operation multiply them to 39. Yet to factor 26 we must iterate 1x39, 2 nil, 3*13 4 nil 5 nil ... 38 nil. More individual operations and on a larger number are required to factor a large number as compared to only one operation to multiply the two primes which compose that large number. Moreover, the larger composite number will almost always have more digits than the two smaller prime factors which compose it.

Good explanations of public key cryptography can be found on the internet with a diligent search. Public key cryptography is the basis of bitcoin. However, public key cryptographs can be subjected to known plain-text attacks by generating cribs using the public key: I encipher text from the public key and use those as cribs to try to determine the private key. Similarly, private keys are only as secure as the media they are stored on. Port scanning, man in the middle attacks, and various viruses all make private keys vulnerable to interception and seizure.

Rather than explain in detail how to generate private and public keys I point you to good tutorials on the topic.

http://www.undefined.com/ia/2015/10/07/a-step-by-step-walkthrough-of-public-key-cryptography/

http://travistidwell.com/blog/2013/09/06/an-online-rsa-public-and-private-key-generator/

https://en.wikibooks.org/wiki/Cryptography/A_Basic_Public_Key_Example

https://medium.com/@tikiatua/symmetric-and-asymmetric-encryption-with-javascript-and-go-240043e56daf

https://www.memresearch.org/grabbe/cryptnum.htm

http://logos.cs.uic.edu/340%20Notes/rsa.html

2.3.5 TRANSPOSITION CIPHERS

Transposition ciphers involve transposing the text. For example, if I wanted to encipher "Where do correct ideas come from?" using a three column transposition cipher the result would be

```
WHE
RED
OCO
RRE
CTI
DEA
SCO
FRO
MXX
```

The enciphered text would then read as

WRORCDSFMHECRTECRXEDOEIAOOX

If instead we used a column key of five scrambled as 4 2 5 3 1 the result is

ERICRHOEEMMROTSFWDRDOOECCAE

Transposition is as seen a simple cipher and thus vulnerable. Still, in combination with other ciphers (e.g. encipher a vigenere text and then transpose it using keyed columnar transposition as K4 of Kryptos might do) the result is a tougher cipher to break - and one more layer of verification for our financial cipher system.

2.3.6 ONE TIME PADS

One time pads are perhaps the most secure cipher. In a one time pad the key 1) does not repeat itself in any discernible fashion 2) is longer than the enciphered message 3) is only used one time and then discarded 4) generally for very short messages (the shorter the better) with few or no repeating elements. If these four features are observed and the one time pad key is not intercepted or known by "Eve" the message is computationally perfectly secure.

For example this pad:

```
QDCMYXTMCZTJAWYOSHDK
JVFXZGPKTFRNSIKDVOLW
GFLPHBTUZDBZQNIIXELP
RUHAUXSPPJJNTZCEJEHP
RJHVJJIZMJPEYXJUKFXX
QFJULYWDUPWHNIKAGPID
WNZGYXEFMYRRGKIQCXFH
TZQJVKUEPXHMEJBPIBOX
TCPFREHPPSVJEBVHPRZF
LHTNXRSQVCNJOWQLLPKM
NBBGUCSOCEWPCQDTFLPB
YJHOQVEWRPVBYSZXOQLV
EISHUKXASRETFULMCTZC
ENKFMOGMTGECPMKDKLAA
WLTYEVFYIJNJBJCXJAIZ
JDGWQVNAKTFMIAOAFHVC
BTRPOJOUTCHZZPHGVYRR
```

Enciphers this text, stripped of punctuation spaces and capitalized:

Lead the people with administrative injunctions and put them in their place with penal law, and they will avoid punishments but will be without a sense of shame. Lead them with excellence and put them in their place through roles and ritual practices, and in addition to developing a sense of shame, they will order themselves harmoniously Confucius

Into this result:

```
BHCPREXBGNIUESGHZHGWRINPSXPDBAVVFRE
QXHTKTXLCKQNNSKFLYABPBMCECUJEQFLWEN
WNEKCAJRKIYNFRRUTZHXXHNRWCCMJBDYBVF
RSLFAXLJQDHUJBDORMYCLJXTYDVROITVEJT
PHJQZHWIAILZGNBCLQIQMJTRZRAWTAMYPBX
LIYQTFNAELCWIVPQAWPKLWEBMPUJIYUSBFM
JPFTLMNZCUMMLJUGSLZCBBQWMPSEQNLIELN
RBYOZPETLOQTMGGQFOQHSYTTXQQCUYXCWYC
KYYSGDZQ
```

Provided the one-time key is never disseminated this message is computationally unbreakable. This is because the key has no discernible pattern, no repetitions, and thus any plain-text may be derived from the cipher-text and the key is never reused. Shorter messages are more secure in any case.

These methods can of course be combined: a one time pad, used to encipher a coded text, which in turn is embedded into an image or sound as a steganograph.

2.4 Cryptographic Vulnerabilities

Here I expose the various vulnerabilities of ciphers and codes to being broken. As seen, some ciphers are more secure than others.

The most effective attacks on a cipher system generally focus on acquiring the key or code book. This generally involves some combination of of deception, eavesdropping, theft, or extortion such as blackmail, hostage taking, and/or threats of violence, possibly including torture. If any of that seems bad to you you are right! However, if you want a real dilemma just ask who would rather see win? The bad guys - or the worse guys? Is it more important to support the bad guys or oppose the worse guys? This is why financial cryptography may be more attractive: it's only a matter of money, not a blood sport. Violence is less likely, profit likelier.

Methods which do not rely on "social engineering" focus either for example on determining the cipher key ("key recovery"), intercepting the message ("man in the middle") or on brute force attacks wherein the enciphered message is derived by an exhaustive iteration of every possible decrypt thereof. Every cipher in principle, including asymmetric ciphers, can be cracked by a brute force attack. However, an effective cipher seeks to make the brute force computational attack so time consuming as to be useless. Brute force attacks can however be optimized using "cribs": known plain-text to cipher-text combinations (the "known plain-text attack"). Cipher-text and the keys thereof may also be vulnerable to a frequency attacks, which seek to infer the key or text based on the frequency of character combinations in the natural language in use by "Alice" or "Bob".

3. ELEMENTS OF REBUS CIPHERS

Rebus ciphers have tended to be ignored in Western literature,[2] because Western writing systems, including Arabic ones, do not use rebus as a writing principle. However, Chinese, and by extension Japanese, both use rebus writing systems.

In alphabetical systems, letters are no longer pictorial depictions of words. A B C and D no longer represent "ox house camel door", etc. as they once did. Instead, the letter has a distinct sound and combinations of letters together indicate the sound of a word without however indicating in and of themselves what the word means. This is entirely different to rebus writing, wherein the written word generally does not indicate its sound but rather indicates its meaning.

3.1 PICTORIAL ELEMENTS OF REBUS

Rebus systems in their simplest and most original form feature symbols which are pictorial representations of actual objects or concepts. An arrow to point a direction is an example easily seen by Westerners. In Chinese, most pictograms are viewed from the front, though with standardization and simplification some characters are rotated 90 degrees and looked at on their side; least frequently, some are pictures viewed from the top. This aspect of that language is not systematized. The picture or symbol bears no indication how the word is pronounced. Such a system enables texts to be written which can be understood by people speaking different languages. This explains why Chinese or Japanese person can get at least a rough idea of texts in the other language, depending on their own intelligence and literacy despite the fact Japanese is unrelated to Chinese linguistically - they are different language families with very different grammars. Japan adopted Chinese symbols for their own writing system. It also explains why one written language can be used by the various dialects of Chinese (principally Mandarin and Cantonese, but also Hokkien, Fouzhounese, even Shanghainese though Shanghainise is falling into disuse).

One problem with rebus is not all ideas can be illustrated with pictures or graphic symbols like arrows. Meanwhile, as civilization grew more complex invention and trade led to a growing number of new words. Rebus writing has techniques to expand on its "base" of pictures (e.g. a picture of an eye) and symbols (e.g., an arrow). By combining these pictograms, complex characters are developed which indicate all kinds of words. This process of combining characters to form new words can be compared, albeit roughly, to spelling in alphabetic languages. There are about 214 root "radical" characters (words), which can be combined like an alphabet to form other words.

The majority of Chinese characters are thus complex composites of characters such as radicals and determinants rather than simple pictures. Sometimes these complex characters are combined with a view to visual memory, as a new picture. These complex characters are generally composite characters composed of at least one semantic element and one phonetic element. These are called phono-semantic characters. Phono-semantic characters use at least one characters to indicate the meaning of the word and another to provide information about the sound of the world. This combination of phonetic and semantic elements is used to coin new ideograms.

3.2 Semantic Elements of Rebus

Restated, one way to expand the number words to cover things which cannot be illustrated easily with a simple pictograms is to use complex characters composed of several elements. A semantic character does not necessarily give information about pronunciation but does indicate something about the meaning of the character.

One semantic element is a set of symbols which indicate general categories such as "fiery things", "metal things", "things you see", "things you eat", "things you say" etc.: these symbols are called determinants. Determinants do not directly indicate how the word is pronounced. Meanwhile, through standardization and simplification, the number of root characters in Chinese is about 214 different radicals. Although there are as many as 80,000 different characters in Chinese (one for each word) there are only 214 radicals. Having memorized 214 characters and about 50 determinants derived therefrom one may then in principle form all other Chinese characters: all Chinese characters are composed of some combination of the 214 radicals.

When used to indicate the meaning of the word a character component of a complex character, whether a determinant or radical, is known as the semantic element of the ideogram.

3.3 Phonetic Elements of Rebus

Another way to expend the pictograms is to use one of the pictograms which sounds like some other word to indicate the sound of the word. This is called the phonetic element of a character. If we know the pictogram which looks like a man standing on two feet and sounds like "ren", and means "person" we can combine the "ren" character with a classifier for things you say to form the first syllable of the word "renshi" - recognize. We use another symbol "shi" for the second syllable, which likewise uses the classifier for things you say as its semantic element coupled with a picture of a person's mouth and sound waves moving forth from it as its phonetic element. The second syllable "shi" of the word "renshi" is thus formed using "zhi" as its phonetic element. Possibly due to language drift historical "shi" became contemporary "zhi".

Sometimes, but not always, phonetic and semantic elements reinforce each other so that the semantic element may also indicate some aspect of pronunciation or the semantic element may indicate some aspect of pronunciation of the word represented. Renshi is the meaning of "know" in the sense of recognize, "I know him", this too explains the choice of the person radical as phonetic element.

Chinese is a tonal language. Thus, there are many words which are homonyms in Chinese. Consequently, the scribes had choices about which character to choose for a phonetic element: in this sense the phonetic and semantic element can be seen as reinforcing each other as in the example of renshi, where the ren character implies that this is the knowledge of persons and things (recognize) as opposed to abstract theory (episteme), wisdom (phronesis), or practical knowledge (metis).

In any event: 认识 means "ren shi" to recognize; to know, as a person (connaitre, kennen). The determinant for things you say (shuo), the character for person (ren) as a phonetic element, the determinant for things you say repeated plus the character a mouth, and waves of sound coming forth from the mouth as a phonetic element (zhi) to remind us the pronunciation (shi) (and perhaps also that we "only" know some people and do not know others; zhi means "only").

Sometimes the phonetic elements do not perfectly reflect the sound of the character borrowed. Chinese has had writing for over 5000 years. Language drift is inevitable over such a long time. Some phonetic elements only provide indication as to how the initial sound of the word is to be said (like "D" as in "Door") or the final sound of the word ("or" as in "door"). This enables modernity to have a good idea how ancient Chinese was spoken. Ancient Chinese can be read by modern Chinese people, unlike even Middle English by Anglophones. Barring catastrophe it is likely that ancient Chinese will be able to be read thousands of years from now.

Mandarin Chinese does not or no longer appears to have a structural logic explaining whether a phonetic element is indicative of the entire exact sound, or merely refers to the initial or final sound ("d as in door" versus "or as in door"). Sometimes phonetic elements only indicate initial, or final sound and the tone of the word may not reflect its phonetic element. Tones are equivocally indicated in the Chinese writing system using sound-alikes. Again, due to language drift tones are not always reflected in current Chinese pictograms. Fortunately, Chinese tones are not of much interest cryptologically speaking.

3.4 REBUS CHARACTERS' STRUCTURE

Rebus writing also has a structure: generally the semantic determinative goes to the left, less frequently to the right, less frequently below or above the phonetic element: semantic components tend to be on the "outside" of the character and the phonetic elements (pronunciation) tend to appear to the interior, i.e. "inside" the character.

3.5 Transliteration using Romanization

Rebus systems generally can be transliterated into Western writing. The most known transliteration systems of Chinese are pinyin and Wade-Gillis. Pinyin is a more accurate exposition of Chinese pronunciation. Although some pinyin letters do not correspond to English sounds they do correspond to sounds of Latin letters in other languages. For examples, pinyin Z equals German Z for example; X equates roughly to Ibero X. Likely some Pinyin corresponds to French transliteration of Vietnamese sounds, a language unfortunately outside my ambit.

The US experience with Japanese ciphers in the Second World War shows that Japan tended to use transliteration of its own writing into Latin characters which were then enciphered. However, there is no reason a cipher system could not use Chinese characters or rebus principles. Indeed I suggest using such symbols and ciphers as one more layer of verification of information in digital financial instruments.[3]

4. Ideal Properties of a Digital Payment System

J. Orlin Grabbe, tended to view private digital currency as a competitor to the governments he hated and as tools to enable money laundering and drug dealing. Grabbe was no lawyer and his lack of knowledge of the law limited his understanding of the possibilities of digital finance.

It is unfortunate that he turned his intellect to foolish endeavors, enabling criminal money laundering, drug dealing, and tax evasion thereby. Rather than thinking about digital finance from an anti-government pro-crime perspective it will prove more profitable and sustainable to think about digital finance in terms of ideal properties of digital finance in a rule of law system.

The problems facing a cryptographic system for digital finance are similar to, yet simpler than, those facing a cryptological system for combat operations. The problem is simpler because less information needs to be transmitted in a more secure environment against fewer and less sophisticated hostiles. The sender and receiver in most civilian situations can be presumed not to be in threat of death or even danger. Thus, they are less likely to make mistakes or require immediate responses. Rather than transmitting targeting and defensive information in the face of immediate hostile action, financial cryptography is simply a matter of securely transmitting data from one civilian to another.

This different environment implies different paramaters for an optimal cryptographic system. These optimal factors for a financial cryptographic system follow:

1) Data must be provable before a court of law. The emitter must always be able to decipher their initial transmission in a reproducible way.

Unlike a combat cipher, the data in this cipher must be able to be recovered and proven before a court of law. In contrast, combat ciphers need not be deciphered e.g. where a unit is eliminated, let alone be admitted into evidence and proven before a court of law. This limits our use of certain cryptologic methods, e.g. classified methods for generating and factoring very large primes or other one way functions that are currently computationally intractable. Likewise, a field agent might use and then discard their one time pad or destroy their cryptological tools. Financial cryptography does not enjoy the luxury either of destroying its own tools or abandonding its own compromised assets.

2) Data must not be deciphered by third parties

Although the ultimate payer ("emitter") must be able to demonstrate their lawful obligations in court, third parties must not be able to defraud the emitter. This is similar to military cryptography, wherein the combatant does not want its opponent to read or spoof its transmissions.

3) Encryption and decryption should be computationally tractable

Military ciphers at times require speed above security. Financial cryptography may have less time pressure and thus face fewer clerical errors. However, less time pressure may also make financial cryptography more vulnerable to being broken. Unlike an artillery fire for effect mission, which must execute properly within minutes, financial transactions may be open to attack for days or even longer.

Computational tractability is maintained using complex cryptography and by limiting the size of the encrypted message.

4) Transmitted information should be as brief as possible so as to limit efforts at decryption

Computational tractability is maintained using complex cryptography and by way of limiting the size of the encrypted message. Limiting message size is also advantageous since that limits the chances to break the encryption: longer messages are easier to break.

5) Redundancy:

The system should use redundant codes and cipher systems to verify its data and avoid frauds. These redundant systems should include a steganographic chop as one more verifier of initial payee (emitter). Redundant systems should also include rebus ciphers, since these are least likely to be effectively analyzed by Western cryptologists. Likewise, the plain-text of the financial instrument can redundantly reiterate itself as keys to the various ciphers used.

ThiEVEs have an incentive to defraud and face no deadly or even violent immediate consequences. However, they are less sophisticated and less organized than state actor. Thus we can anticipate a larger number of low powered attacks by a variety of actors against financial cryptographs as compared to military cryptography.

In military cryptography the attacker is generally large, well funded, sophisticated, coordinated, but monolithic, i.e. unique. In contrast, in financial cryptography there will be many attackers most of whom will be unsophisticated and uncoordinated. Since the time constraints on cryptography are much relaxed in the financial setting, the same information should be enciphered and encoded redundantly, using multiple channels, to avoid fraud and forgery. Redundant systems ensure the correct party is paid and that the payer cannot be defrauded. Redundant systems also ensure that even if the attacker can break one cipher to forge a financial instrument that they will be unable to break all the encryption used permitting a public proof before a court of law that the instrument is forged or fraudulent.

Examples of methods of redundancy include using a steganographic "chop" as one more verifier of the emitter, payee, and amount to be paid. Likewise, plain-text indicia on the instrument can also be used as steganographs for enciphered information or as keys to the ciphers used in the instrument. To make a light-hearted joke to prove the point, an emitter might self-designate as "Bank of AM ERICA".

As noted our ideal message should be as brief as possible to limit efforts at decryption or forgery. Financial Transaction Data is limited to a few fields ("slots") namely:

1. pay to:
2. amount (including monetary unit e.g. $, Eur. Yen, etc.)
3. transfer date:
4. SWIFT/BIC - Bank Identifier Code
5. IBAN/ROUTING NUMBER/CTC
6. Account Number
7. Signature Block
8. Notes:

These data slots are few in number, limiting computational intensity of encryption and decryption and also tending to make the messages more secure: Longer messages are easier to decrypt. In principle the minimal information required is "pay to" and "amount". The additional fields however enable a very flexible use of this instrument, legally speaking.

5. Legal Aspects of Crypto Currency: Problems and Possibilities

The late James Orlin Grabbe is the principal theorist of crypto-currency[4] He authored innovative articles and programs to create a "digital monetary trust" the forerunner of bitcoin, and not coincidentally wrote extensively about many of the issues facing bitcoin and protocols thereof (proof of work, double spending problem, e.g.).

Although J.O. Grabbe was a great economic thinker he was no lawyer. This, and his libertarianism, explains why he ignored certain legal issues which both make bitcoin less than ideal as a digital financial instrument and which should be considered by authors of digital financial instruments and digital financial software. These legal disadvantages of crypto-currency follow.

5.1 Problems Facing Legal Enforcement of crypto-currency Transactions

A key problem of crypto-currency is the enforcement of claims involving crypto-currency before courts. People who complain about the state, it's taxes and rules, inevitably wind up in legal conflicts. Those legal conflicts are often with other private persons. It is entirely likely one of those parties to a legal conflict, ideology notwithstanding, will seek legal redress from the very state against which they so bitterly complain.

Problems with legal enforcement of crypto-currency claims include:

1) simply identifying the parties to the transaction

2) ascribing jurisdiction, i.e. determining which court may hear the claim and which national law to apply to the transaction

3) the unavailability of equitable remedies for crypto-currency transactions,

4) the statute against frauds, and

5) refusal of the court to intervene to parties in pari delicto.

I go into detail on the non-jurisdictional problems facing crypto-currency claims below.

5.1.1 EQUITY UNAVAILABLE FOR CRYPTO-CURRENCY CLAIMS

Equity is an exceptional discretionary remedy offered by the court in the interest of justice. Equity is not a personal right of the parties. It is a corrective of the law imposed by the court in the interest of justice. Equity looks ex post, whereas law (lex scripta) looks ex ante. Equity is only offered as an exception, and only in the discretion of the court: there is no right to equity. However, though equity is discretionary there are principles which govern its application. These are called "equitable maxims".[5]

The most important maxim of equity is "he who seeks equity must do equity".[6] Likewise, "he who comes into equity must come with clean hands."[7] These two maxims imply that equitable remedies will likely be unavailable for claims over crypto-currency.

It is entirely possible that the court will regard the very use of a crypto-currency to be inequitable, because crypto-currency fosters illegal and immoral conduct such as money laundering, tax evasion, the drug trade, and human trafficking. To be offered the remedy of equity the party seeking the equitable remedy must not only be lawful - they must also be equitable, i.e. not fraudulent, not in bad faith nor outright criminal. Since crypto-currency fosters illicit behavior it is likely courts will refuse to offer equitable remedies for crypto-currency transactions.

5.1.2 In Pari Delicto

Crypto-currency claims may also meet no court remedy due to the principal that the courts will, between two wrong-doers, offer no remedy: they are in pari delicto.[8] Where two wrong-doers seek the remedy of the court the court will not intervene on behalf of either wrong-doer.[9]

5.1.3 Statute of Frauds

The statute of frauds provides that a contract for land or an interest in land, a contract to marry, or a contract which cannot be completely executed within one year or which is worth more than the statutory sum (currently in the USA: $500 by laws of the several states) must have a writing signed by the party against whom that contract is to be enforced memorializing the agreement.[10] The entire contract need not be in writing. However, there must be a writing memorializing the agreement signed by the party to be held liable for their agreement. The writing may be digital and the signature too may be digital: one's name in their email has been found to be an adequate "signature" to satisfy the statute of frauds.[11] Likewise, 15 U.S. Code § 7001 regards digital contracts and digital signatures as enforceable in cases of international and interstate commerce. However, crypto-currency contracts may not meet the statute of frauds since crypto-currency transactions are in principle anonymous. There is no signature nor even name identifying the party to the (possibly illegal) transaction. Thus it is doubtful that the court would find the necessary "signature" to satisfy the statute of frauds.

5.1.4 COURTS REFUSE TO ENFORCE OR REMEDY ILLEGAL CONTRACTS

Related to these problems is the fact that bitcoin as the currency of choice for all kinds of illegal transactions will often be implicated in unenforceable contracts. Illegal contracts for gambling, prostitution, and other mala prohibita might not lead to criminal prosecution. However, the illegality of an underlying contract does not entail a right to set aside resulting property transactions. The property transfer resulting from a purported contract for gambling or prostitution will generally not be set aside by the court because of the illegality or unenforceabilty of the underlying contract. Although the underlying contract might be illegal and unenforceable, the property transaction's validity is independent of the rights and duties created by the purported contract.[12]

If there are real legal problems facing claims revolving around crypto-currency how might digital financial instruments be issued, which are also enforceable whether at law or equity?

5.2 Possibilities of Lawful Enforceable Digital Financial Instruments

5.2.1 Commercial Paper (Negotiable Instruments)

In earlier writing, I have fairly extensively examined the problems of digital currency as a case of securities fraud and counterfeiting. The fact that the primary purpose of bitcoin is to evade taxes, launder money and buy and sell illegal goods and services (drugs, guns, human trafficking) explain why government will eventually ban bitcoin, likely by banning bitcoin exchanges and refusing to enforce contracts or disputes around bitcoin.

This is not to say that there are no licit purposes for digital financial instruments. There certainly are. Here I address digital financial instruments as a variety of commercial paper.

Commercial paper is a legal instrument which makes an unconditional promise to pay a sum certain by a definite date in legal tender: thus, bitcoin cannot be a negotiable instrument.[13] Examples of commercial paper include promissory notes, checks, and money orders.

Commercial paper may be distinguished as "order paper" which is indicated "pay to the order of John Doe" i.e. pay to the order of a specific person. "Order paper" may be endorsed by the payee and thereby turned into bearer paper. Bearer paper is indicated using terms like "Pay to the order of cash" "Pay to the order of bearer". Bearer paper may be negotiated by any person bearing it. Order paper may be negotiated only by the payee until endorsed.

There is an obvious possible market for digital commercial paper, which in my opinion is underexploited.

5.2.2 Intellectual Property

5.2.2.1 Patent

It is unlikely a patent of a cipher would be enforceable. However, ciphers can well be protected as trade secrets. Similarly the name given to a cipher might also be trademarked.

Patent is likely unavailable for most cryptographic systems since they generally will be obvious extensions of prior art[14] and fail to meet the test of novelty. Moreover, ciphers and algorithms are likely too general to be a proper subject of patent.[15] Patents must be novel, not obvious extensions of prior art, and must not be abstract mere ideas like algorithms.

Even if patent were available for a cipher it is not the best form of intellectual property protection. Patenting a cipher requires divulging the entire protocol for the cipher to the government. This both compromises the cipher's security and also subjects the cipher to possible government appropriation due to classification thereof as a national security secret. Furthermore, patent is only valid for about a dozen years. After the patent expires, the patented information becomes public domain. Patent, even if it were available for abstract ideas like algorithms, is not the optimal IP protection for a cipher system.

5.2.2.2 Trade Secret

Instead of a futile, expensive, and sub-optimal search for non-existent patent protection, authors of cryptographic protocols would better seek protection of their intellectual property as a trade secret. So long as a trade secret is maintained in secrecy it is valid. That is, trade secrets are potentially perpetual.[16] Trade secret law is primarily state law; however, the common law here is largely codified in the US States by the Uniform Trade Secrets Act.[17] A federal private cause of action does exist for interstate and international violations of trade secret law.[18]

5.2.2.3 Trademark

Similarly, trademarking the name of the cipher is another way to obtain intellectual property over one's cipher system. Although "Reproducible Rebus Super Cipher(TM)" is not trademarked, clever names of secret ciphers have some marketability. US Federal trademark law is defined in the Lanham Act[19] which essentially codifies the common law. A steganographic image could for example also be a trademark.

5.2.2.4 Recordation

A final method of protecting one's cipher system while also enabling it to be proven is to use recordation thereof. Ordinarily we record only interests in land. However, contracts, wills, and other legally operative documents may be recorded. The advantage of recordation of parts of the cipher system, e.g. public keys, is that it enables provable recovery of the enciphered information in the event of a legal dispute. Provable authentication of the cipher system is thus obtained without exposing the entirety of the cipher system, maintaining the cryptographic protocols as a trade secret and enabling court victory. Since few people know about recordation or where the information might be recorded by the clerk the likelihood of a hostile person recovering parts of the cipher system through indexing records is diminished. Since redundant ciphers and codes are used, even if e.g. the public keys of asymmetric cryptographic elements of the cipher are recovered by legal inquiry the secret portions such as private keys remain computationally non-trivial.

5.2.2.5 Choice of Law Clauses

Digital financial instruments may also include information regarding the governing law of the instrument and/or places where the instrument may be lawfully enforced. These are known as contractual choice of law and choice of jurisdiction clauses respectively. Thus for example "This instrument is governed by the law of Hong Kong, People's Republic of China", "This instrument may be enforced before the courts of Singapore, only" etc. In this manner Chinese persons or persons working in or with China may obtain common law rules to garner greater confidence in the financial instruments generated.

Conclusion

Crypto-currency faces real legal problems: securities fraud, counterfeiting, money laundering, compliance with the above regulatory regimes; but also the question of substantive remedies at law for purported contracts or equity for immoral transactions. At the same time, the need for micro-credit liquidity in the poorest parts of the world and the fact of kleptocratic regimes and failed states explains why private digital financial systems have beneficial as well as malevolent aspects. Here, I have described a series of cryptographic protocols for secure yet legally sound digital finance. Rather than seeking to appropriate currency seignorage or to finance frankly illegal transactions to undermine state power, digital financiers would be better to seek sustainable business models, some of which were suggested here.

About The Author

Dr. Eric Engle LL.M. (Humboldt) earned law degrees in the United States (JD, St. Louis, ROTC scholarship) France (DEA, Paris II), and Germany (LL.M., Humboldt, LL.M.Eur. Dr. Jur. Bremen) He passed the New York bar on his first attempt. He has taught law in France (Nanterre), Germany (Bremen, Humboldt), Moscow, Russia (Pericles), Estonia (Tartu) Ukraine and Bosnia (Fulbright). These review quizzes are edited, revised, and written by him

© Eric Engle

Learn more at www.amazon.com/author/quizmaster

OTHER BOOKS BY ERIC ENGLE

Eric Engle has written and edited dozens of books reviewing all basic law courses and the actual questions from the 1992 and 1999 bar exams, released by the NCBEx. Available at:

http://amazon.com/author/quizmaster

He also offers free law review articles online and free online search engines for US, French, German, Russian and International law at

http://mindworks.altervista.org

Dear Reader,

I hope you enjoyed this book or found it useful. If you did I would really appreciate you posting a review on Amazon. I read all reviews personally to improve the product.

You can also write me an email at eric.engle@yahoo.com for specific questions or for clarifications. You want to learn and I love to teach and I will do my best to answer. Your review is important.

Thank you for your support!

REFERENCES

http://www.undefined.com/ia/2015/10/07/a-step-by-step-walkthrough-of-public-key-cryptography/

http://travistidwell.com/blog/2013/09/06/an-online-rsa-public-and-private-key-generator/

http://acrigs.com/FRAVIA/stego.htm

https://en.wikibooks.org/wiki/Cryptography/A_Basic_Public_Key_Example

https://medium.com/@tikiatua/symmetric-and-asymmetric-encryption-with-javascript-and-go-240043e56daf

https://www.memresearch.org/grabbe/cryptnum.htm

http://logos.cs.uic.edu/340%20Notes/rsa.html

1 Eric Engle, *Bitcoin: Digital Finance Law* 69-85 (2017) https://www.amazon.com/Bitcoin-Dr-Eric-Allen-Engle/dp/1544784783/ref=asap_bc?ie=UTF8 (examines counterfeiting, money laundering, tax evasion. stock fraud and crypto-currency).

2 "Note that among living languages Chinese presents special problems not only for the cryptologist but also for the Chinese themselves. No Sinologist knows all the 80,000 or so Chinese symbols, and it is also far from easy to master merely the 9,000 or so symbols actually employed by Chinese scholars. How far more simple it is to use only twenty to twenty-six symbols! Since Chinese is a monosyllabic language, it seems almost hopeless to try to write Chinese by the sort of mechanism used in an alphabetic polysyllabic language" NSA, "The Friedman Legacy" Sources in Cryptologic History Number 3, page 19 (2006)

3 See, e.g. David Kahn, "Why Weren't We Warned?" 4/1 Military History Quarterly, 50, 54-55 (Autumn 1991).

4 I expose and discuss Grabbe's ideas about digital finance extensively in Eric Engle, *Bitcoin: Digital Finance Law* 1-68 (2017) https://www.amazon.com/Bitcoin-Dr-Eric-Allen-Engle/dp/1544784783/ref=asap_bc?ie=UTF8

5 *See generally* Eric Engle (ed.) *Equitable Remedies* Quizmaster Point of Law Review (Volume 8) 51-52 (2015). https://www.amazon.com/Equitable-Remedies-Subtitle-Quizmaster-Review/dp/1515132374/ref=asap_bc?ie=UTF8

6 Koster v. (American) Lumbermens Mut. Casualty Co., 330 US 518, 522 (1947)

7 Precision Co. v. Automotive Co., 324 US 806, 814 (1945).

8 *See, e.g.* Bateman Eichler, Hill Richards, Inc. v. Berner, 472 U. S. 299 (1985).

9 *See, e.g.* Pinter v. Dahl, 486 US 622 - Supreme Court 1988.

10 *See, e.g.*, Wilson Floors Co. v. Sciota Park, Ltd., and Unit, Inc. 377 N.E.2d 514 (1978).

11 *See,* Cloud Corp. v. Hasbro, Inc., 314 F. 3d 289 (Court of Appeals, 7th Circuit 2002).

12 *See, e.g.* Ryno v. Tyra, 752 S.W.2d 148 (April 28, 1988).

13 Eric Engle (ed.) *Negotiable Instruments*, Quizmaster Point of Law 27-28 (2014).
https://www.amazon.com/Quizmaster-Point-Law-Review-Instruments/dp/1515076725/ref=asap_bc?ie=UTF8

14 "the subject matter sought to be patented and the prior art are such that the subject matter as a whole would have been obvious at the time the invention was made to a person having ordinary skill in the art to which said subject matter pertains." § 103 of the Patent Act of 1952, 35 U. S. C. § 103 (1964 ed.).

15 "Laws of nature, natural phenomena, and abstract ideas are not patentable". Alice Corp. v. CLS Bank International, 573 U.S. __, 134 S. Ct. 2347, 2354 (2014); Bilski v. Kappos, 561 U.S. 593 (2010).

16 Kewanee Oil Co. v. Bicron Corp., 416 U.S. 470 (1974).

17 Uniform Trade Secrets Act *available at:* http://www.uniformlaws.org/Act.aspx?title=Trade%20Secrets%20Act

18 Defend Trade Secrets Act (DTSA), 18 U.S.C.§§1839

19 15 U.S.C. §§ 1051-1127.

www.ingramcontent.com/pod-product-compliance
Lightning Source LLC
Chambersburg PA
CBHW030512220526
45464CB00006B/2759